THE LITTLE BOOK of EXPERIMENTS

THE LITTLE BOOK of EXPERIMENTS

Edited by **Sophie Duncan** and **Alice Bell**

Hodder & Stoughton
A MEMBER OF THE HODDER HEADLINE GROUP

British Library Cataloguing in Publication Data
A catalogue record for this title is available from the British Library

Orders: please contact Bookpoint Ltd, 130 Milton Park, Abingdon, Oxon OX14 4SB. Telephone: (44) 01235 827720.
Fax: (44) 01235 400454. Lines are open from 9.00–6.00, Monday to Saturday, with a 24-hour message answering service. You can also order through our website *www.hodderheadline.co.uk*

ISBN 0 340 875 917

First Published 2002
Impression number   10 9 8 7 6 5 4 3 2 1
Year   2008 2007 2006 2005 2004 2003 2002

Copyright © 2002 NESTA Enterprises Ltd

All rights reserved. This work is copyright. Permission is given for copies to be made of pages provided they are used exclusively within the institution for which this work has been purchased. For reproduction for any other purpose, permission must first be obtained in writing from the publishers.

Designed and typeset by Julie Martin Ltd.
Printed in Great Britain for Hodder & Stoughton Educational, a division of Hodder Headline Plc, 338 Euston Road, London NW1 3BH.

Contents

Acknowledgements	6
Foreword by Stephen Twigg	7
Planet Science – Where science comes to life	8
Science Centres	9
Health and safety	11
Links to other organisations	12
Which crisps are the saltiest?	14
Choccy Rocks	17
Pop-Pop Boats	21
Illusory Pendulum	23
Hot Mouse	25
Clucking Cups	27
Electricity and Magnetism	29
Up, up, up and away…	31
Make your own sunset	33
Forever blowing bubbles…	35
Where's hot and where's not	37
The stupendous sciZmic school-pond project	39
Growing crystals	41
Mini Water-world	43
Give it a pasting	45
Bad-breath!	46
Cereal Chemist	47
Make a fossil	48
Custard gone Crazy	49
Dancing Paper	50
Goose-pimples	51
Ketchup Sachet	52
Magic Milk-bottles	53
Make a Menagerie	54
Rotting eggs and rotten teeth	55
It's a Gas!	56
Blowing in the Wind	57
Planetary Plates	58
Pinhole Camera	59
Pressurised Plastic	60
Light Fantastic	61
Whether the weather will…	62
The Great Boat Race	63
Seed-tastic!	64

Acknowledgements

Planet Science would like to thank The AstraZeneca Science Teaching Trust for its support of this project.

We would also like to thank all those people who contributed their experiments, including those whose experiments appear on the website. We are sorry we could not include them all.

Foreword

This book is packed full of engaging and innovative demonstrations and experiments you can do with your pupils. *The Little Book of Experiments* has been put together with the support of teachers, science centres and scientists. All the experiments have been tested and work really well either in the classroom or at home. I am really grateful to The AstraZeneca Science Teaching Trust for sponsoring the book.

We know the benefits of engaging children in science from an early age, and hope that this book will really help intrigue and excite the children in your class. Some of the activities have been specially designed to bridge KS2 and KS3, a critical point in any pupil's career. Whilst the book caters primarily for KS2, a website of activities for all ages and Key stages accompanies the book, providing teachers with a resource which we hope will grow as you add your own ideas to our database.

You may have come across some of these experiments before. But we hope there are some new ones that you can either use in the classroom or ask the pupils to do at home with their parents. We would love to hear your stories of how the experiments went and any ideas you have for new experiments. Let us know how you get on by contacting Planet Science at *www.planet-science.com*

Planet Science – Where science comes to life

If you've enjoyed these experiments and demonstrations and would like to try some others, there's an extensive online collection at *www.planet-science.com/sci-teach*. Most are suitable for KS2 and KS3 classes, and a few would make interesting demonstrations for KS4 students. The database is easy to search and when you've found the activity you want, you can print off the instructions and hand them out to pupils, colleagues and parents.

And while you're there...

Planet Science is committed to supporting the transition between KS2 and KS3, and the Association for Science Education has developed a 'passport' to help make the bridge between these two stages as easy as possible. The passport consists of a set of downloadable pages which look like our own EU passports, but the visas the KS2 child collects represent their knowledge of various scientific concepts, terms and experiments. This means that when they arrive at secondary school, their new science teacher can immediately gauge their existing level of scientific understanding.

http://www.planet-science.com/sciteach/passport

If you navigate your way to the **Out There** area of the Planet Science site, you'll see a link to 'SciKids'. In here, you can read about some of the legendary figures that have shaped science today. Follow Galileo as he ponders the Universe, learn about Jagadis Chandra Bose and his revolutionary botanical investigations, and join Edison as he develops a host of ingenious inventions. Inspiring stuff!

http://www.planet-science.com/outhere/scikids

Perhaps even more important though in motivating young people are today's scientists and technologists. And that's where **Next Steps** comes in.

In this area of the site, visitors can take the 'Suits You!' quiz – a semi-serious personality test that will help determine which area of science you might be most suited to working in. And when you've done that, you can check out some real life careers on the 'Meet Your Match' database. We've hand-picked a huge range of young(ish!) scientists and technologists and persuaded them to fill in a questionnaire detailing just what they do all day, their career path and advice they'd give to others – and even which celebrity they reckon should play them in the movie of their life! Whether your interest is in engineering buildings, forensics, sports technology, science journalism, or laboratory investigations into the 'paranormal', you can get the lowdown here…

For personal careers advice, visitors can email the Planet Science team of advisors and they'll respond within 2 working days.

http://www.planet-science.com/nextsteps

After all that, what about a spot of light relief for your hard-working pupils? **Wired Up** is packed with games, quizzes and activities. For starters, they can take a voyage of adventure with 'Planet 10'. This is a highly addictive and exciting 3-D adventure – and their knowledge of the solar system will increase dramatically in the space of a few games… Other games have less science content, but are fun all the same! And the quiz archive can be used to turn any spare 15 minutes into 'Who Wants to be a Sci-Zillionaire?'

Finally, check out the CD-ROM of resources for primary science education. This was specially created for Science Year by the ASE, and every school was sent one this summer. If yours went astray, don't worry, the material can also be found online at *www.sycd.co.uk*

Science Centres

Science centres have huge resources to engage and enthuse your pupils. Find out about your local science centre at *www.scienceworlds.co.uk*. This easy-to-navigate website includes all the information you need to find out about the science centres near you.

Several science centres have offered their expertise to help us with the book. This page lists those centres and highlights some information about them. Why not pay them a visit?

The Magna Science Adventure Centre is a 'Science Adventure Centre'. At Magna, scientific principles sit side-by-side with art, design, technology, industry, environment and lifestyle issues. Visitors create their own 'adventure' through hands-on challenges.

Address: Sheffield Road, Templeborough, Rotherham, S60 1DX
Tel: 01709 720 002
Website: *http://www.magnatrust.org.uk*

Techniquest in Cardiff contains 160 exciting hands-on exhibits. They include puzzles, challenges, and scientific marvels to enthuse and amuse everyone. Schools can book visits and benefit from the excellent programme of exciting science shows and planetarium demonstrations.

Address: Stuart Street, Cardiff, Wales, CF10 5BW
Tel: 029 20 475 475
Website: *http://www.techniquest.org*

The Science Museum has a world-class collection of objects, some highly interactive galleries, and a programme of drama, shows, science sleepovers and workshop activities. The museum claims that if you spent only a minute with each of their exhibits you'd be there over a month.

Address: Exhibition Road, South Kensington, London, SW7 2DD
Tel: 020 7942 4777
Website: *http://www.sciencemuseum.org.uk*

The Museum of Science and Industry in Manchester has just opened a brand new re-vamp of their hands on gallery, 'Xperiment'. Visit this, along with their other exhibits including planes, trains, automobiles and a reconstruction of a Victorian sewer system.

Address: Liverpool Road, Castlefield, Manchester, M3 4FP
Tel: 0161 832 2244
Website: *http://www.msim.org.uk*

London Zoo was the world's scientific zoo, opening in 1828. Until 1847, it kept the public out and existed for academic research alone. Since then it has firmly established itself as one of Britain's most famous visitor attractions. See, talk to, hide from (and smell!) the 650 species of animals, and visit the amazing new 'Web of Life' exhibition.

Address: Outer Circle, Regent's Park, London, Greater London, NW1 4RX
Tel: 0207 722 3333
Website: *http://www.londonzoo.co.uk*

At the **Royal Air Force Museum**, Hendon you can marvel at legendary planes and great hands-on exhibits all displayed over the 15 acres of the historic former Hendon Aerodrome at RAF Hendon, one of the oldest aviation centres in the country. If your pupils like planes, this is the place to take them.

Address: Grahame Park Way, Hendon, London, NW9 5LL
Tel: 01902 376200
Website: *http://www.rafmuseum.org.uk*

The Making Place is exactly what the name suggests – a place for visitors to explore scientific or technological ideas in order to design and make a product to take away. The emphasis is on learning all about scientific principles through the process of designing, making and evaluating technological application.

Address: 3 Exmoor Street, London, Greater London, W10 6BE
Tel: 020 8964 2684
Website: *http://www.themakingplace.co.uk*

Remember, this list is not comprehensive. Check out your local centre at *http://www.scienceworlds.co.uk*

Health and Safety

Health and safety during science lessons is important.

Science can be amazing, but sometimes to be so amazing you need to do things that are out of the ordinary, and use unfamiliar and unstable ingredients, equipment and/or methods.

However there is no reason to be scared. School science is extremely safe, and by taking a few simple precautions you can minimise the risk. Serious injuries to students are about a hundred times more likely in PE than they are in science!

When carrying out the experiments in this book, please note where we have made reference to sections of the ASE publication *Be safe!* (3rd edition, 2001.) Every primary school should have at least one copy of this publication, or it can be obtained directly from the ASE (see reference on page 12).

When tackling the experiments in the book we recommend teachers take into account all possible safety considerations (not just the ones we have highlighted), and are familiar with the whole of the latest edition of *Be Safe!*.

Pupils have to be aware of their own safety too. Not just because they will be carrying out experiments, but also because risk assessment is a key part of the science curriculum. This is seen at KS2 in Sc1 2e – 'use simple equipment and materials appropriately and take action to control risks' – and it is a consideration that will affect your pupils throughout their education – primary school, KS3, GCSEs, A-levels or GNVQs, and university.

Health and safety, and risk assessment are key parts of any science work, but are also relevant to other areas of your pupils' lives. They need to be equipped to make sensible decisions. So it's worth starting early, which makes it (of course) a key job for the primary school teacher.

For more information, please consult the *Be Safe!* guidelines. The CLEAPSS School Service will be able to help with anything more. (See pages 12–13 for details of this organisation.)

Links to other organisations

This page outlines what support, advice and information is available to help teachers make science lessons more exciting and relevant.

The British Association for the Advancement of Science (BA)

Education activities include:

- National Science Week – a week of over 2500 science activities, experiments and science discussions across the country.
- BAYSDAYS – children's science festivals full of workshops, dramas and hands-on activities.
- Support and resources through the BAYS award schemes for KS1–3.
- Activity packs and newsletters to members, with more activities and information on science events.

All activities can be found on *www.the-ba.net*

SciZmic

SciZmic, the Science Discovery Clubs Network, brings science clubs together to participate in events for schools. For information go to *www.sciZmic.net*

The Association for Science Education (ASE)

Professional body for those involved in science education at all levels from pre-school to higher education, including technician members. It has a national network of teachers, lecturers, advisers and a team of permanent staff providing a unique service. The ASE provides:

- Advice and guidance on specific problems and issues.
- PSR for suggestions about primary science teaching and Education in Science for news.
- Specialist ASE publications and commercially published books all at discount prices to members.
- An Annual Meeting with more than 300 events over three days.
- Professional development opportunities at all levels.

As its major contribution to Science Year, ASE created an innovative series of CD-ROMs and online resources sent to schools for KS2/3. You can access downloadable versions of the CD-ROMs at *www.sycd.co.uk* or go to *www.ase.org.uk* where you'll find more information.

The AstraZeneca Science Teaching Trust

Go to *www.azteachscience.co.uk* for information and professional development in primary science teaching and KS2/3 projects.

The CLEAPSS School Science Service

- Provides resources on health and safety, equipment and anything to do with practical science and technology. All education authorities in the UK (outside Scotland) are members so you can have free access to these resources. Go to *www.cleapss.org.uk* for more information.

- A helpline for teachers covering everything you wanted to know about teaching science in primary schools but were too afraid to ask! Call them on 01895 251 496 or e-mail, *science@cleapss.org.uk*

Science Line

Free science information service answering questions on all aspects of science, technology and medicine. Call them free on 0808 800 4000 (lines are open 1pm–7pm Monday–Saturday). You can find more information at *www.sciencenet.org.uk*

The Qualifications and Curriculum Authority (QCA)

A guardian of standards in education and training.

- Go to *www.qca.org.uk* for access to a wide range of information on general education issues around curriculum and assessment.
- The National Curriculum Online (*http://www.nc.uk.net/*) outlines the science curriculum with links to relevant websites as well as support and guidance on how to teach science to gifted and talented pupils, and pupils with learning difficulties.
- The National Curriculum in Action website (*www.ncaction.org.uk/subjects/science/index.html*) uses pupil case studies to show how national curriculum science works in practice.

The Science and Engineering Ambassadors Campaign (SEAs)

- Brings enthusiastic science and technology professionals to schools to inspire young people about science and technology.
- Co-ordinated by the Science Engineering Technology Mathematics Network (SETNET) through it's SETPOINTS. Contact your local SETPOINT at *www.setnet.org.uk* for more information.

The Royal Institution (RI)

- Communicates science to the general public by lectures and experiments.
- Series of science events for KS2+ and online resources for teachers and pupils based on their lectures.

Go to *www.rigb.org.uk* for more.

The Institute of Biology (IOB)

- A professional body for UK biologists that supports science educators by organising competitions, events and courses as well as giving schools posters, CD-ROMs and a newsletter to help you help your pupils.

For more information and advice go to *http://www.iob.org*

The Royal Society of Chemistry (RSC)

- Wide range of activities for pupils, including a national chemistry competition and chemistry at work events.
- Offers training and produces curriculum material designed to provide teachers with stimulating ideas for practical work in the classroom. *www.chemsoc.org/learnnet/* has more information.
- A book, *That's Chemistry*, was sent free of charge to all UK primary schools in 2001 and contains stacks of experiments and ideas for lessons. Details at *http://www.chemsoc.org/networks/learnnet/thats-chemistry.htm*

Which crisps are the saltiest?
A real investigation to get the whole class thinking

Setting the scene

This very open-ended investigation really stretches the pupils' investigative skills that are extremely important in KS2–3 transition. It provides an excellent opportunity to get the class comparing and evaluating different methods of investigating the same topic.

The pupils are told their teacher has high blood pressure. The doctor has ordered a diet as low in salt as possible. But the teacher *likes* salted crisps so which brand would be the healthier one for him/her to eat?

Now give them the challenge. Using their imaginations the pupils work as scientists to create ideas of experiments they could do. They then choose an experiment to try to find the best type of crisps for their teacher.

Other than that, there is no right or wrong way of doing this. The pupils' imagination is better than ours!

You will need

- Bags of ready-salted crisps (at least three different varieties),
- A range of equipment that KS2 pupils will be familiar with.

As it is up to your pupils to design their own testing strategy we can't predict exactly what they will need.

Instructions

A few ideas you can suggest, hint at or highlight (not to mention have equipment set up and readily available for) are:

- Use a microscope to try to count the grains, or at least the grain density (perhaps the Science Year Intel microscope).
- Look on the packet/label for nutritional information.
- Carry out a taste-test with a sample of people.
- Wash the salt off the crisps, filter, evaporate the filtrate and weigh or observe the residue.

Further information

There is no explanation for this experiment, as it is about encouraging the pupils' scientific imagination, but it can easily be slotted into other work on topics of health and nutrition or more general chemistry.

Extension ideas

Obviously setting up a microscope will take a lot longer than just looking at the labels! If one group finish quickly, they can always do a different test and then compare the two different experiments afterwards. This can be extended to encouraging the groups to come up with ideas they could not conduct in a classroom but which might also work.

At the end of the lesson, ask the groups to report back. As a whole class, compile a list of all the ideas and then get the pupils to compare their methods (e.g., is the nutritional information better than a taste-test, which relies on different people's definition of what is 'salty'?)

This experiment was recommended to us by...

Peter Borrows from CLEAPSS. It was used as one of the Challenges in the Annual Primary Science Challenge in Waltham Forest in the early 1990s.

National Curriculum links in KS2

The entirety of Sc1 can be covered through this (especially 1a, 2a and 2b). It also links to Sc2 2b and 2c.

Looking forward – National Curriculum links in KS3

Again, most of Sc1 can be covered by this investigation, especially 'ideas and evidence in science' (Sc1 1a–c) along with planning (Sc1 2a and 2c–e) and evaluation (Sc1 2o–p) skills. It can also be used to address the topic of 'nutrition and diet' (Sc2 2a).

Remember BE SAFE: If taste-testing is involved (officially or otherwise) good hygiene is important! (*Be Safe!*, 3rd edition, section 6)

Which crisps are the saltiest?

Your teacher has high blood pressure. The doctor has ordered a diet as low in salt as possible.

But your teacher *likes* salted crisps – so which brand would be the healthier one for them to eat?

Part 1 Discuss the problem in your group and come up with five different ways for comparing the amount of salt in different crisps.

1
2
3
4
5

Part 2 Choose one of these five ideas and write up a plan for how you could make it into a fair test – you need to put enough information so someone else could do the experiment again themselves just by reading what you have written.

Equipment List:

Method:

Part 3 Let your teacher check your method. Then get testing and record the results.

Brands of crisps tested:

Result:

Which crisps are the saltiest?

Part 4 Compare your testing method with the other people in the class – which was the best idea?

The Little Book of Experiments © 2002 Hodder & Stoughton Educational

Choccy Rocks

Act like a geologist — a very hungry one — and identify 'rocks' using chocolate

 ## Setting the scene

The pupils are astronauts who have just arrived on a strange new planet. They are trying to find clues about their surroundings from the rocks scattered around them. Half were produced on the surface of the planet from cooled molten rock, half came from outer space as meteorites.

The aim is to match the chocolate samples to the rock descriptions shown in the table. If they get it right, they can eat the rock.

The Little Book of Experiments

You will need

Chocolate Sample ('rocks')	Rock description
Milky Way	A meteorite with a 'fusion crust'
Rocky Road*	A 'chondritic' meteorite
Solid milk chocolate	An iron meteorite
Aero	An igneous rock from an explosive eruption
Chocolate Brownies*	An igneous rock that cooled *slowly* as a magma
'Mint Crisp' chocolate bar	An igneous rock that cooled *quickly* as a magma

* These you'll need to prepare yourself. The recipes are on the next page. You can do this alone or with the pupils. The advantage of the latter is that it can give the pupils a feel for the history of the rock as cooking is quite a good analogy for rock formation (although it doesn't take nearly as long!) There are lots of great ideas linked to this on *www.planet-science.com*

Instructions

Get the pupils to work in groups of six. Give each group a plate with a small square of each of the 'rocks'. Emphasise that they must **not** handle the samples. This would contaminate the evidence (and mean they can't eat them afterwards!).

First get them to draw detailed pictures – their 'field notes' – of the samples, with labels to describe both the inside and outside of the 'rocks'. Encourage them not to use food words like cake or chocolate. *Handy Hint:* Get the pupils to 'spot the differences' between the 'rocks'.

The worksheet we've included in the book gives the students the description of the rocks and four clues to help them work out which is which.

When the group has identified all the samples, they each get to eat one of the 'rocks'.

This experiment was recommended to us by...

Paula Martin, a post-graduate student at the Department of Geological Sciences, University College London.

National Curriculum links in KS2

Sc3 1d, also obtaining and presenting evidence (Sc1 2e–h), and most of considering evidence and evaluating (Sc1 2i–m).

Looking forward – National Curriculum links in KS3

Geology is greatly developed in the KS3 Sc3 curriculum. This experiment underpins much of the section on 'geological changes' (Sc3 2d–f), especially if you take the opportunity to cook the 'rocks' with the students, thereby simulating geological processes. As with KS2, aspects of Sc1 curriculum can be covered, especially planning and obtaining evidence (Sc1 2c–d and 2f–h) and considering evidence and evaluation (Sc1 2k–m).

Remember BE SAFE: Good hygiene is important – ensure the students clean their hands carefully beforehand and handle the chocolate as little as possible! (*Be Safe!*, 3rd edition, section 6)

Choccy Rock recipes

Re-create billions of years of natural history from the comfort of your own kitchen, as you discover the bubbles and 'chondrules' that can make the insides of meteorites and earth-formed rocks all lumpy.

Meteorites
a-k-a Rocky Road Chocs

400 g (14 oz) chocolate pieces (melted)
100 g (4 oz) marshmallows

- Line a small but deep tin with aluminium foil and pour in about half the melted chocolate.
- Add marshmallows, and mix until coated.
- Pour remaining chocolate over the marshmallows and spread flat.
- Refrigerate until cold.
- Remove some cubes for samples, but keep the rest intact.

Igneous Rock
a-k-a Brownies

50 g (2 oz) cocoa powder
200 g (7 oz) self-raising flour
250 g (8 oz) soft margarine
300 g (10 oz) caster sugar
4 eggs
200 g (7 oz) glacé cherries
100 g (4 oz) chocolate drops

- Pre-heat oven to Gas Mark 4/180°C/350°F.
- Sift cocoa powder and flour.
- Cream sugar and margarine together.
- Beat in eggs, adding a little of the flour mixture each time.
- Fold in remaining flour mixture, cherries and chocolate drops.
- Spread the mixture into a tin and bake for 30–60 minutes, checking constantly.
- Cool before slicing.

 Remember BE SAFE: Good hygiene is important, and you must be careful about allergies!
(*Be Safe!*, 3rd edition, section 6)

Choccy Rocks

You and the rest of your group are astronauts.

You've just arrived on a strange new planet and are trying to find clues about your surroundings from the rocks scattered around you.

Part 1 Examine the rock samples you have been given. **Remember you must not touch the samples with your hands.** This would contaminate your evidence (and mean you can't eat them afterwards!)

Draw a diagram of each of the rocks, and label features of both the insides and outsides of the rocks.

Part 2 Each of your rocks matches to one of these types of rock:

- A meteorite with a 'fusion crust'
- A 'chondritic' meteorite
- An iron meteorite
- An igneous rock from an explosive eruption
- An igneous rock that cooled *slowly* as a magma
- An igneous rock that cooled *quickly* as a magma

You need to work out which is which. Use the clues below to help you, and match your rock samples to the right title. Write the title of the rock on each of your diagrams.

Some **meteorites** have a crust. This forms when the rock is heated as it enters the Earth's atmosphere. The outer part of the meteorite melts and forms a **fusion crust** (which often has marks and indentations).

Magma is hot, molten rock and comes to the planet surface when a volcano erupts. When the magma cools down it makes **igneous** rocks. As it cools, crystals form in the rock – the faster the magma cools, the smaller the crystals are.

The insides of some meteorites can be quite lumpy, with small round pieces called chondrules. This type of meteorite is called a **chondritic** meteorite.

As magma rises from underground to the Earth's surface it releases bubbles of gas. If these gases are released very quickly, **explosive eruptions** occur (just like opening a fizzing drink after shaking it up). These bubbles can leave their imprint on a volcanic rock, leaving it like a frozen sponge with lots of holes in it.

The Little Book of Experiments © 2002 Hodder & Stoughton Educational

Pop-Pop Boats
Make your own steam-propelled nautical engine

Setting the scene

Trying out this 'pop-pop boat' helps the pupils think about propulsion and can be linked to history lessons on Victorian transport. The technical term for the engine that propels the boat is a pulsating water engine (PWE). They are believed to have been invented by Thomas Piot in 1891.

You will need

- Foil tray (or something that floats),
- 20–25 cm copper tubing (about 3 mm internal diameter),
- Dowel (or something else round and about 1–2 cm in diameter),
- Modelling clay,
- Pipette or dropper,
- Small candle (tealight) and match/lighter,
- Tub of water to launch your boat on.

Instructions

- **Firstly you need to prepare the boat.** Bend the front of the foil tray to form a prow (the front bit), then pierce two small holes in the back of the tray (the stern). The holes should be a few centimetres apart.

- **Next make your engine.** Wrap the copper tubing around the dowel rod about 5 or 6 times to make a closely-wrapped coil, leaving about 3 cm of straight pipe at either end. These straight bits at the end will be the engine's inlet and outlet. Remove the coil from the dowel rod.

- **Now put the two together.** Push the straight ends of the coil through the holes at the back of the boat so about ½ cm of the tubing sticks out at the bottom. Seal up any space around the tubing with modelling clay so the hull doesn't leak.

- **Finally, fill up the engine.** Turn the boat upside down and using the pipette squirt some water into one end of the copper-coil engine.

- **Ready to Go!** Place the boat on water and rest the lit candle under the coil. Once the water you squirted into the engine has heated up, it should start to move!

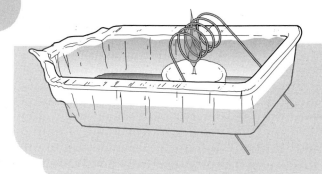

The Little Book of Experiments

Further Information

You need to know Newton's Third Law of Motion: 'For every action there is an equal and opposite reaction'.

This means that if you push something, it'll push back at you just as much. Think about swimming – you push the water backwards with your arms and you go forwards; if you want to go faster you push faster. It's 'equal' because it's the same amount of force; it's 'opposite' because it's in the other direction.

The coil's acting like a boiler, making steam which gets forced out of the bottom of the boat through the copper tube. The water pushes back at this steam and so propels the boat forwards.

After the steam is ejected, a partial vacuum is created in the tubing thus forcing more water to be sucked into the boiler, starting the whole process over again – a really simple steam engine (or 'water impulse engine' if you want to sound techie).

This experiment was recommended to us by...

Dr Allan Paterson of the Magna Science Adventure Centre, near Sheffield.

National Curriculum links in KS2

Sc4 2d and 2e. Also can be linked to the history curriculum – 11a (Victorian Britain).

Looking forward – National Curriculum links in KS3

Again, much of the curriculum relevance for this experiment is found in the 'forces and motion' section of Sc4. Although this experiment is perhaps not appropriate to the quantitative relationships the KS3 curriculum calls for, it qualitatively underpins ideas of speed, distance and time (Sc4 2a), balanced and unbalanced forces (Sc4 2c) and pressure and forces (Sc4 2g).

Remember BE SAFE: Take precautions with all flames in case anything goes wrong, and be very careful about handling anything hot! (*Be Safe!*, 3rd edition, section 8)

Illusory Pendulum
Play with your mind and learn about the eye

Setting the scene

This effect was described by a German astronomer called Pulfrich who was blind in one eye. But you need two eyes for the trick… so perhaps he got the idea from his assistant.

You will need

- Two eyes (both your own),
- String,
- White modelling clay,
- Dark filter (cheap sunspecs split in two will do).

Instructions

- With the string and a blob of clay, make a pendulum that swings in a straight arc across your line of sight.
- Sit about two metres away to view the swinging blob. It should be swinging across you – left, right, left, right…
- Now place a dark filter over one eye, and look at the pendulum again. Amazingly, the pendulum will seem to swing in and out as well as across in an elliptical orbit – round and round and round…
- Put the dark glass on the other eye – the pendulum's orbit reverses direction.

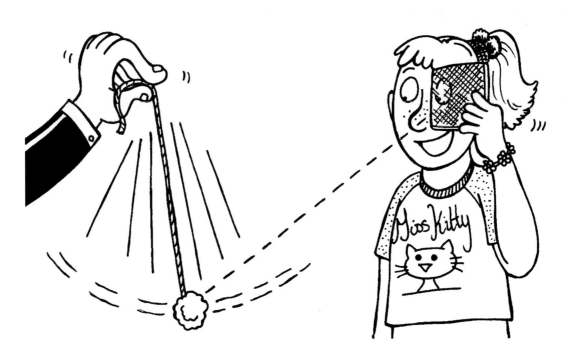

To Measure the Magic

- Do the experiment over a desk.
- Without the dark filter on, place some sort of marker (e.g. a pencil stuck to a desk with plasticine) just under the centre of the pendulum's left-right-left-right swing.
- Now put the filter on again, swing the pendulum and put a second marker where you think the centre of the round-and-round-and-round swing is.
- Use a ruler to measure it – the illusion in depth can actually be greater than the physical sideways swing!

Further information

When you cover your eye with a filter it becomes more sensitive to light. The pupil gets bigger to allow more light in, and the signals to the brain are delayed slightly, to allow more light to enter the eye (just like a camera with a slower shutter speed).

The eye with the dark glass sees the moving pendulum delayed in time and therefore in a different position from the other eye. The brain puts the two positions together, fooling you into thinking the blob is moving in and out in an ellipse. This is similar to when 3-D films put two images together to fool you into thinking things are coming out of the screen.

Extension ideas

Try filters which allow differing amounts of light through (perhaps using one or more filters on the eye together).

This experiment was recommended to us by...

Professor Richard Gregory FRS from the Department of Experimental Psychology, University of Bristol. He's also famous for his many highly successful books and work with 'hands-on' science centres, most notably founding the Exploratory, Bristol.

National Curriculum links in KS2

Sc4 3d, giving the explanation links to aspects of 'ideas and evidence in science' (Sc1 1a–b).

Looking forward – National Curriculum links in KS3

Similarly to KS2, senses are not really present in the curriculum at KS3 but there are links to the 'behaviour of light' topic (Sc4 3a–f). The use of historical examples links well to Sc 1a–c.

Planet Science

Hot Mouse

Learn at little about animals without the smell, mess and rota for who takes them home at weekends...

Setting the scene

The initial stage is quite simple to run, and lets the pupils use their imagination as they construct a nest for a 'mouse' (really made out of a small medicine bottle).

The best thing about the experiment is that after this first activity it can be taken in all sorts of directions. Follow-on activities present a host of opportunities for teachers who want to use their imaginations.

You will need

- Straw,
- Boxes,
- Thermometer,
- Water,
- Small medicine bottle (one with a childproof lid).

Instructions

- **Make your 'mouse'** – fill the small medicine bottle with warm water (use the thermometer to ensure it's at 37°C). This simulates a small mammal such as a mouse or vole.

- **Set the challenge** – the aim of the pupils' experiment is to design a mouse nest that will be effective at keeping the mouse warm. Pupils are given straw and once they have made their nests they place them outdoors in suitable mouse hiding holes.

- **Testing the results** – After an hour, retrieve the bottles, open them and measure the water temperature to see how successful the nests have been in keeping the little 'mice' warm.

The Little Book of Experiments

Extension ideas

You can use the nest building to discuss insulators (perhaps trying the experiment again with other materials than just straw). Or you can develop lessons on hibernation and environmental conservation.

There are also huge opportunities for developing data handling of results or using electronic equipment such as digital thermometers. Depending on age range, spreadsheets and graphing activities are also possible.

This experiment was recommended to us by...

Louise Fieldgate, a PGCE student in Farnborough.

National Curriculum links in KS2

Sc2 5a, Sc3 1b, and the whole of Sc1 can be covered depending on how the planning process and evidence is treated.

Looking forward – NC links in KS3

Again, this relates to aspects of Sc2, particularly in terms of 'living things in their environment' (especially Sc2 5c). As with KS2, the investigation is ideal for thinking about the thermal conductivity of materials, except that in KS3 more chemical vocabulary is used (Sc3 1d). The experiment has links to aspects of Sc4 relating to the idea of conservation of energy, which is introduced to pupils at KS3 (in Sc4 5d–g). As with KS2, most of the Sc1 investigative skills curriculum can be covered.

Clucking Cups
Explain the amplification of sound without making too loud a noise!

Setting the scene

In this activity each student makes their own musical instrument – a 'clucking cup' – to explore what sound it makes and how to manipulate it. This toy is very simple to make, and we've included a couple of fun extension activities.

You will need

★ Fishing line or smooth string (it's worth trying a few different types to find the best and avoid unleashing a bad brand on the pupils),

★ A plastic cup (yoghurt pots work too),

★ A damp cloth (most work but, again, it's worth testing as you prepare the lesson),

★ Tape or modelling clay.

Instructions

★ Cut a length of string about the height of the cup.

★ Stick the string to the centre of the inside of the cup with the tape or the clay. Turn the cup upside down. The string should hang down inside the cup.

★ Draw the damp cloth along the length of the string. This starts the string vibrating as the cloth slips and sticks – just like a violin bow.

Further information

Vibrating a piece of string in the same way with a damp cloth produces a sound, but it is very quiet. Adding the cup to the end of the string creates a larger surface to vibrate, amplifying the sound. How does this work? Is the string sufficiently exposed for the damp cloth to be drawn across it?

 ## Extension ideas

Do exactly the same as above, but with a bucket. Or better, a variety of different sized buckets, with bowls and cups and even bins. If you can get a really giant bin (half a metre in diameter) you get a really deep noise that sounds more like a cow than a chicken!

These cups are ripe for decoration, get the class to add beaks and eyes to their clucking cups – if you want to be really scientific about this you can find pictures of chickens and get the students to examine what a chicken looks like to copy the features.

 ## This experiment was recommended to us by...

The Education team at the Techniquest Science Discovery Centre in Cardiff.

 ## National Curriculum links in KS2

Vibration of sound (Sc4 3e–g). Areas of Sc1 can be covered in extension activities, as can aspects of the Art and Design curriculum.

 ## Looking forward – National Curriculum links in KS3

The KS3 curriculum on vibration and sound (Sc4 3i–k) is similar to the KS2, except that more scientific terms (such as amplitude) are introduced and the concept of frequency and pitch is addressed, both of which can be covered by this experiment. As with KS2, areas of Sc1 can be covered in extension activities.

Electricity and Magnetism

This very famous experiment lets us tell a story, so concentrate – here comes the history bit...

Setting the scene

Electricity and magnetism are linked. In fact, electricity causes magnetism. Danish scientist Hans Christian Oersted discovered this in 1819. It came as a bit of a surprise to him, as he made this discovery while teaching students that electricity and magnetism have nothing to do with each other!

As fable goes Oersted accidentally put a compass near an electric current and the compass needle moved. Compasses always point north, so either his lecture room had moved (which is just silly) or there was a magnet around to mess it up. But when he looked he couldn't find any magnets, so the only thing that could have affected the compass was the electrical current. He experimented a bit more and decided magnetic fields were produced by an electric current.

That's all very well, but could it work the other way round? That was the question that faced Michael Faraday in 1831. Re-create his experiment 21st century style with help from Dr Jonathan Hare from the BBC's *Rough Science* programme.

You will need

- Sticky tape and insulation tape,
- Sandpaper,
- Cardboard,
- Reel of insulated copper wire (about 50 m),
- Small strong magnet,
- Any LED,
- Film canister.

Instructions

- Cut out two cardboard circles about 50 mm in diameter, each with a hole in the middle. The holes need to be big enough for the film canister to fit snugly inside it.
- Space these card rings about 1 cm either side of the centre of the canister. Hold them in place with insulating tape.
- Leaving about 10 cm of wire free at either end, wind the wire round and round and round (and round) the film canister between the card rings. It needs to have 500–1000 turns, so you might like to do 20 and then pass it round a group.
- Sandpaper off the insulation from the last 5 mm or so of each end of wire and connect it to the LED (solder if possible).
- Pop a small (but powerful) magnet into the film cannister, secure the lid and shake. The LED will come on – you've generated electricity from moving a magnet!

The Little Book of Experiments

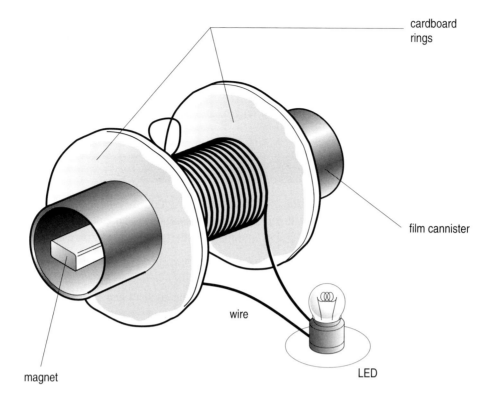

Further information

Putting the magnet into the tube doesn't work (try if you like) – you need the magnet to be moving. Devices like this turn movement energy from wind-farms or steam-powered turbines into transportable electricity. This is why you can switch on a light in Norwich even if the energy source is actually in Cornwall.

This experiment was recommended to us by...

Michael Faraday! OK, not really... it was produced with advice from Dr Frank James, an expert on Faraday from the Royal Institution where Faraday worked for many years. This particular version of how to make the experiment was designed by Dr Jonathan Hare, University of Sussex.

National Curriculum links in KS2

'Ideas and evidence in science' (Sc1 1a–b).

Looking forward – National Curriculum links in KS3

The connection between electricity and magnetism as addressed in this experiment is not specifically within the KS3 curriculum, but it crucially underpins understanding of much of the 'electricity and magnetism' section of Sc4 (Sc4 1d–f) and the topic of 'energy resources and energy transfer' (Sc4 5a–g) which is introduced at KS3. Again, this also links to 'ideas and evidence in science' (Sc1 1a and 1c).

Up, up, up and away...
Make a Hot Air Balloon

You will need

- Tissue paper,
- Sheet of thick paper/card to make template,
- Water-based glue,
- Scissors,
- Something to heat the air (e.g. hair dryer).

Instructions

Ready...

- First, sort out your tissue paper. You will need four sheets. It can be whatever colour you like (two different colours will make lovely stripy balloons).
- Lay the sheets out 'landscape' style (that is longest edge horizontally) and fold in half, lengthways.
- The balloon's going to be made out of four sections. You need to make a template out of card so that each section is the same (the guidelines for the template are shown in the diagram).

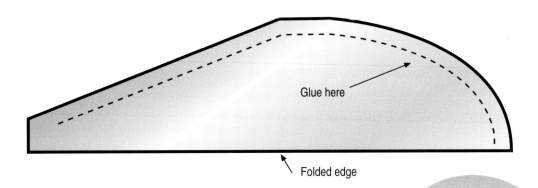

Steady...

- Copy this shape onto each of the four folded tissue paper sheets. The straight line at the bottom needs to run along the folded edge of the sheet (so you could open it up butterfly-style to make a balloon shape).
- Cut out the shapes. Throughout this process be very careful not to tear the tissue paper, if you do, seal any holes up very carefully or replace the sheet completely – you don't want any leaks!
- Glue them together, one by one. Be careful not to tear the tissue paper, and leave enough space open at the mouth for the hot air source.

The Little Book of Experiments

...Lift-off!

- ○ Check your balloon over for any potential leaks, the edges must be sealed properly and it's best to wait until the glue is dry.
- ○ Place the mouth of the balloon over your hot air source to fill it with hot air.
- ○ The hot air is lighter than the air around it – you'll feel the balloon start to pull up slightly against you, when you trust its ready to float, let go…
- ○ **WARNING:** don't overheat the balloon, paper is very flammable!

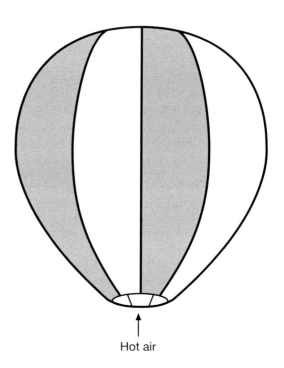

Hot air

 ### Extension ideas

There are several factors that affect a balloon's performance, try out different balloons and compare them.

You can try out different sizes of balloon, and different shapes are worth experimenting with too. Giant tubes are funny (made with rectangular sheets of paper, no need for a template!) – and they've been known to swallow up small people as they land.

Try comparing different heat sources – hair dryers, popcorn makers, convection heaters – but be careful with all of them because you do not want to overheat the balloon, **paper is flammable**. Be careful not to let the balloon touch the hot air source.

 ### This experiment was recommended to us by...

The Explainers in the hands-on galleries at the Science Museum, London.

 ### National Curriculum links in KS2

Sc3 2b, Sc3 2c. Extension activities can be linked to most of Sc1.

 ### Looking forward – National Curriculum links in KS3

The fact you are changing the 'state' of the air to make it hotter and so less dense links to aspects of Sc3, especially the sections on 'solids, liquids and gases' (Sc3 a–b) and 'physical changes' (Sc3 2a–c). The 'flight' of your balloons also can be linked to the relationship between force area and pressure (Sc4 2g). As above, extension activities can be linked to much of Sc1.

 Remember BE SAFE: Never use a heat source that has naked flames or exposed red hot wires. Any electrical equipment must have passed the portable electrical appliance test, even if it's been brought in from home! (*Be Safe!*, 3rd edition, sections 5 & 10

Make your own sunset

Why is the sky blue? Why is the sunset red? Make your own mini-universe and all will be revealed

Setting the scene

This teacher demonstration explains that age-old children's question – why is the sky blue? There are also extension activities that let the pupils play around with colour mixing themselves.

You will need

- A model sun (use a slide projector – instead of a slide, use a large piece of aluminium foil with a small hole in it),
- A model atmosphere (a large jam jar or 500 ml beaker, water and milk),
- A screen (an A4 sheet of paper with some method of holding it in place, e.g. blue-tac),
- A model universe, (any reasonably dark room will suffice).

Arrange the equipment so that the light from the projector passes first through the beaker before focusing on the screen. If you are feeling artistic at this point, add silhouettes of palm trees, a sparkling beach, a few exotic birds etc. to the screen.

Instructions

- Add water to the jar until it is $3/4$ full. Check that the beam of light goes through the water before focusing on the screen.
- At this point, no colours are seen on the screen. This is because our model atmosphere is too clean! The real atmosphere contains dust.
- To mimic the dust, slowly add milk to the jar whilst stirring the mixture. As the water becomes more cloudy, the spot on the screen will become orange, then red.
- Even though the light on the screen is orangey-red, the 'atmosphere' in the jar will appear blue where the light passes through it.
- The image on the screen is what you see when you look at the sun.

The Little Book of Experiments

Further information

White light is a mixture of all the colours of the rainbow. Small particles (such as dust) scatter the light in all directions, but blue light is scattered more efficiently than red light.

The blue light is scattered away by the particles in the solution and into your eyes so the solution looks blue. This leaves the orangey-red light to shine through onto the screen.

The same effect also occurs if mist, light cloud or smoke partially blocks the sun. The effect is more pronounced when the sun is low in the sky because the light has to pass through more of the atmosphere (hence more dust) before reaching the observer.

Extension ideas

For some really counter-intuitive colour mixing tricks that help underpin the optical effects shown here, try playing around mixing green and red lights. As you'll discover, light behaves differently from paint: red light and green light make… yellow light!

Add blue and this theoretically should make white light – but in practice it does not often work. You can link this to art classes and get the pupils to make colour wheels, which also emphasises the difference between light (additive) and painting (subtractive) colours.

This experiment was recommended to us by…

Dr Roy Lowry, Department of Environmental Sciences, University of Plymouth.

National Curriculum links in KS2

Sc3 2a, Sc4 3a–b (everyday effects of light), Sc4 4b.

Looking forward – NC links in KS3

As with KS2, this experiment links to the curriculum on light, but at KS3 this replaces the more intuitive 'everyday effects of light' topic with 'the behaviour of light' (Sc4 3a–f), which is much more detailed. The experiment prepares pupils well for work in KS3 on colours (Sc4 3e) and filters (Sc4 3f). It also links to the curriculum relating to the workings of the solar system (Sc4 4a–d).

Planet Science

Forever blowing bubbles…
A frothy foam of experiments to investigate the bubble

Setting the scene

These experiments can be done alone or in series to build up knowledge of surface tension, soaps and bubbles.

You will need

- Water,
- Pippette,
- Coin,
- Sticky tape,
- Marbles,
- Glass.

Instructions

Explore surface tension using the following challenges:

- **How many drops of water can you fit on a coin?** Using a pipette carefully drip water onto a coin drop by drop, you'll see that a lot will fit on the top.

- **How many marbles can you fit into a cup that is already full of water?** Get the class to predict how many marbles you can fit in the beaker without it overflowing. Add them one by one.

- **How do those little animals float on water?** Little insects (pond skaters) can walk on water. Fill a tub with water and make your own pond skaters out of sticky-tape folded in half (sticky-side to sticky-side). Let them float in the tub. Then add some soap to the tub – they all fall through.

Further information

The strange behaviour in the three experiments is all down to something called surface tension. Water forms a tight 'skin' around itself. This is what's holding the water in the beaker over all those marbles and on the coin. It's also what keeps the insects on top of the water.

If you add soap you cut down the surface tension and the 'skin' disappears, as the soap gets between the water molecules. The pond skaters drown. Also, if you reduce the surface tension the molecules of water won't be so quick to pull themselves into tight little drops, and you can catch air in them, making bubbles, which is why soapy water can foam but normal water can't.

Extension ideas

Make you own bubble mix

No one can agree on the best bubble mix recipe, but this should serve you well: 1 part washing-up liquid, 4 parts glycerine (available from chemists), 32 parts **warm** water. You can experiment with this recipe and compare different brands of washing-up liquid. There are many different recipes for bubble mix out there, why don't you experiment to find out which is best (look up the bubbles section at *http://www.planet-science.com/outthere* for more info).

Huge bubbles

Make a huge bubble-wand out of a coat hanger bent into circle, with string wrapped round the wire to pick up lots of mix. Don't blow the bubbles – draw the wand through the air and seal the bubble with a twist of your wrist (practice makes perfect).

Giant bubbles

Make a giant bubble wand out of a plastic hula-hoop (wrapped in string). Get a pupil to stand in a paddling-pool of bubble mix and lift the giant wand over them to make a human-bubble!

Cubic bubbles

Bubbles always make spheres. Try bending your coat-hanger bubble wand into different shapes and you'll always get a sphere bubble.

But you can make a cage to trap those bubbles and force them into a different shape. Make a cubic frame out of straws or wire (again, remember to wrap string round each straw/wire).

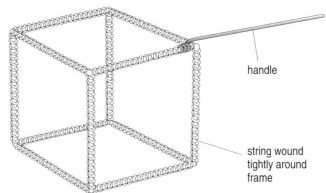

handle

string wound tightly around frame

Dip it in bubble mix – you'll have films stretching from each side making a cross in the centre. Take a straw, dip the end in bubble mix (so it won't pop the films) and blow into the central cross. Hey-presto – one cubic bubble!

This experiment was recommended to us by...

Helen Reynolds, Head of Physics, Gosford Hill School.

National Curriculum links in KS2

Sc3 2a and 2b, most of Sc1 2 (investigative skills) can be covered if you get the class to compare bubble mix recipes.

Looking forward – National Curriculum links in KS3

Many of these experiments link to the 'elements, compounds and mixtures' section of the Sc3 curriculum (Sc3 1c–h), but at KS3 the vocabulary has become much more chemical, and pupils are encouraged to think in terms of materials as arrangements of atoms and molecules. Again, any bubble mix recipe investigations can be used to cover aspects of Sc1.

Where's hot and where's not

Looking for a subject for investigation? Look no further than your own four walls!

Setting the scene

The class is going to investigate the heat in their classroom, where it comes from, where it goes to, how it's wasted, etc. The activity has direct relevance to the pupils' everyday world and helps them develop investigative skills, especially testing predictions.

It is best to do this activity in the morning (before the school warms up with all those sweaty pupils) to get greater temperature differences.

You will need

- Graph paper,
- Pens/pencils,
- Colouring pencils/crayons,
- Data logger (or thermometers to take the temperature of room).

Instructions

- Get the pupils to draw 'bird's-eye views' of the classroom. Ensure they include windows, doors, desks etc. in their diagrams.
- Ask the pupils to predict where they think the hottest and coldest parts of the room are, and why.
- Get them to mark their hot and cold predictions on their diagrams with blue and red colouring pencils (darker where they think the temperatures are most extreme).
- Make a large version of the diagram of your classroom on the board for all to see (but without the hot and cold labelling the pupils did).
- Measure the air temperature in each of the areas the pupils had predicted as particularly hot or cold, and mark them onto the large map on the wall. You may wish to measure the air temperature in other areas of the classroom too.
- Were the children right about where was hot and where was cold? Discuss with the pupils why they think some places were as they predicted and some were not. Have they taken everything into consideration?

Extension ideas

Now you know more about the movement of heat within your classroom get the pupils to draw a new layout of the classroom that makes best use of the hot and cold spots. How can you move desks to take full advantage of the 'free heat' in the hotspots? What can you do to warm up coolspots (e.g. draught-proofing the windows)?

Do the temperatures change over time? Take several measurements over a short period of time, to see how variables affect the heat in the classroom, for example the number of people in the room, what you're studying (e.g. maths versus an art lesson!), or what time of day it is.

The whole school could do the experiment and compare results with different classes whose rooms are in different parts of the building. You could even link with other local schools and do investigations such as old buildings versus modern, or big school versus small. For help linking with other schools use the sciZmic network of science clubs at *www.sciZmic.net* (details on page 40 with the pond-dipping experiment).

This experiment was recommended to us by...

Ann Saffery of Create.

National Curriculum links in KS2

The entirety of Sc1 can be covered through this (especially 1b, 2a, 2c, 2h–m). It also links to Sc3 1b and Sc3 2c. The experiment also covers 'geographical enquiry and skills', especially 2a–b in the Geography curriculum. Also links to Mathematics – including most of Ma3 (space and measurement) and Ma4 (handling data).

Looking forward – National Curriculum links in KS3

This experiment is ideal for initiating the important idea of conservation of energy, which is introduced to pupils at KS3 (Sc4 5d–g). Again most of Sc1 can be addressed with the investigation, and it also links to aspects of the Sc3 curriculum regarding the thermal conductivity of materials (Sc3 1d).

1f, 2a–b and 2e from the Geography curriculum are also relevant here. The links to Mathematics are using and applying shape, space and measures in Ma3. The experiment can be developed to include use of coordinates from Ma3 3e.

The stupendous sciZmic school-pond project

If you have a pond or stream at school or nearby, why not find out about the creatures that live in it?

There are two sections for this – one for beginners and one for those who are already well aware of the delights of a school-pond (and so might like to know about how to develop its use further).

For Beginners

You will need

- A small net (quite tightly woven),
- A tray containing water from the pond,
- A pond (it doesn't have to be in your own playground, and it doesn't even have to be a pond – any largish expanse of water with things living in it).

Instructions

To 'pond-dip', sweep a pond net through the water several times, remove it quickly and put the contents in a tray that already contains some water. Be careful nobody falls in!

Different nets will select different sized creatures, as smaller creatures will pass through the holes. Sweep the net in different areas, and compare the creatures you find (e.g. close to the edge, in the middle, under a tree, along the bottom).

Now you want to investigate that data. Use a magnifying lens or container (or better still your Intel electronic microscope from Science Year) and get the pupils to carefully draw diagrams of the creatures, and use keys to identify them. Pool the data from the whole class to discover how many creatures there are and draw up a table to compare these results with previous and subsequent pond-dips.

Remember to put all the water and creatures back when you have finished observing the creatures!

For more experienced pond users

So you think you've got the best school-pond in Britain then? (*Well maybe it is, but how would you know?*) Or maybe you think yours is rubbish and want some advice from fellow school-pond users? (*But how could you find such people?*) Or maybe you want to give your school-pond greater context by linking the results of your pupils' experiments with those from another environment. (*But how could you possibly find a school to work on pond experiments alongside you?*)

Never fear – sciZmic is here! Link your pond to another following these simple steps…

You will need

- A computer and access to the internet, logged on to *www.sciZmic.com*

Instructions

- Advertise for a pond-partner on the sciZmic discussion board.
- Wait for a reply (hopefully not long…)
- Agree on what your experiment's going to be and how you're going to measure it (remember, for a fair comparison you have to make sure both pond experiments use the same procedure).
- Compare your results.
- Go back to the discussion board to share what you've found out with sciZmic and the rest of the school-pond user community!

National Curriculum links in KS2

Pond-dipping provides opportunity to cover much of Sc2, along with a great way of covering all of Sc1. Outside of science, it relates to much of the geography curriculum and you can cover aspects of ICT. The more you use the sciZmic network to extend and develop the work, the more of these sections of the curriculum you can cover.

Looking forward – the National Curriculum links in KS3

You can use sciZmic (or just the idea of linking your pond-dipping work to other schools) to directly link your pupils' work with the secondary schools in your area – it's a great way of showing off to KS3 teachers quite how well prepared for secondary school science your pupils are.

As above, pond-dipping can be used to cover or augment much of Sc2. In KS3 pupils start thinking on a smaller lever and learning about cells, as well as bringing in more abstract topics such as photosynthesis and the nitrogen cycle. Also as above, pond investigations are a great way of covering almost all of Sc1, and there are geography and ICT applications too.

Remember BE SAFE: About working outdoors, and avoid pond-dipping where access is steep or otherwise difficult! Wash your hands after the activity. (*Be Safe!*, 3rd edition, section 16)

Planet Science

Growing crystals
Explore the beauty of crystal formations hiding in everyday kitchen materials

Setting the scene

Get hold of a magnifying glass to give the class a close look at some crystals of ordinary table salt. Let the pupils examine the shapes of the crystals and sketch pictures of what they see. (You could make use of the Science Year Intel Micropscope.)

They should see that the crystals are small cubes. Now they have examined the salt's cubic crystal structure, the following activity lets them grow their own salt crystals, and make much bigger versions.

You will need

- ★ Table salt,
- ★ Small saucepan and access to something to heat it over (i.e. a kitchen hob),
- ★ Jam jar or clear container,
- ★ Cotton thread,
- ★ Pencil or bit of similarly shaped wood.

Instructions

- ★ Pour half a glass of tap water into a small saucepan.
- ★ Add a heaped teaspoon of table salt to the water and heat the mixture until it's just hot enough for you to keep your finger in it without it hurting.
- ★ Keep adding more salt in small amounts until no more of it appears to be dissolving in the hot water. You now have what's known as a 'saturated' solution of salt. The teacher can always prepare this (not so safe) aspect of the experiment before the lesson.
- ★ Let the solution cool down and pour the cooled contents into a jam jar.
- ★ Balance a pencil across the top of the jam jar, and hang a bit of thread from the middle of it, so that one end of the thread dangles into the water, almost touching the bottom of the jam jar.
- ★ Place the jam jar in the sunlight and wait for a few days until at least half the water has evaporated.
- ★ You should see crystals forming, similar to the ones the class would have sketched when looking at the salt under the magnifying glass or microscope.

Further information

The molecules of table salt (sodium chloride) have started to crystallize out of the solution onto the piece of cotton. They too should be shaped like cubes. If you leave the solution undisturbed for a few days, you'll be amazed at how big the crystals become.

The Little Book of Experiments

In many solids, the arrangements of the building blocks of the material (ion, atoms and molecules) can be a mixture of different structures. In crystals, however, a single type of collection of atoms is repeated over and over again throughout the entire material. For an analogy, you can think of crystals as a big skyscraper, in which all the rooms are built to exactly the same design.

In your salt-crystal skyscraper there are two types of building block, sodium particles (called ions) and chloride particles (called ions). These can be thought of as occupying the corners of each of the rooms, but in a particular way – if you looked closely at the corners of the rooms in the skyscraper, you'd see that alongside every sodium particle there's a chloride particle, and vice versa. You would never see two sodium particles next to each other, and likewise for the chloride particles.

Extension ideas

Many household goods are sold in the form of crystals. Try repeating the above experiment with sugar, Epsom salts (this should make 'spiky' crystals), potash alum or iron tablets (you'll need to crush these first, before you dissolve them in the water) instead of the salt.

Ask your local pharmacist for copper sulphate (which is blue). There are other coloured crystals you might be able to get your hands on as well (crystal growing 'kits' are readily available).

This experiment was recommended to us by...

Dr Mike Bullivant from the Open University – you may also know him from *Rough Science* on BBC2.

National Curriculum links in KS2

Sc3 2a–b, 2d, 3b, 3d. Aspects of Sc1 can be covered, especially if you take the opportunity to experiment with different crystals.

Looking forward – National Curriculum links in KS3

This experiment (especially the explanation that goes with it) sets up superbly the concepts of materials as chemicals, and of chemicals being made up of particles, which are central to the Sc3 curriculum at KS3. It relates to Sc3 sections on 'elements, compounds and mixtures' (Sc3 1c–h) and 'physical changes' (Sc3 2a–c). Again, there is scope to cover aspects of Sc1.

Remember BE SAFE: About handling any chemicals and all heating, especially handling anything hot! (*Be Safe!*, 3rd edition, section 8 & 9)

Mini Water-world
Learn all about the ups and downs of water

Setting the scene

Water is vital to life. It comes out of the sky as rain. But how does it get up there in the first place? And what influences how much of it comes down?

Make a mini-system to see how water gets from the soil up into the clouds and back down again. In fact, make two – one with vegetation, one without. The experiment has to be done over several weeks, so needs some advance planning. It can even be made to last all term – the class's very own pet ecosystem!

You will need

- Two transparent containers with lids, for example large glass pickle jars or plastic tubs (they should be identical to each other),
- Soil with some sand or gravel well mixed in to ensure good drainage,
- Seeds that quickly germinate, such as herbs or beans,
- Water (ideally from a spray bottle).

Instructions

- Place the same quantity of soil in each container – you can measure it out with a cup.
- Moisten the soil by adding equal amounts of water to each container. Make sure it is moist but not waterlogged.
- Leave one container with just the water, but in the other sow the seeds (according to the packet instructions). This container with plants in is known as a **terrarium**.
- Water the seeds in by gently spraying them, then close both systems by putting the lids on the containers.
- Place the containers side by side in a sunny position, but not in direct sunlight.
- Each day look at your containers and note where and how the water appears in them. Is it on the lid and sides of the container? Does the soil still appear to be moist? Does it look like it has been raining? Or does it remind you of other weather conditions?
- Get the class to record their observations, looking out for differences between the two containers and making notes on how warm and sunny it is where the containers are kept.
- Every few weeks the containers may require additional watering. Ensure they receive the same amount.

Further information

The water should evaporate (change from liquid to water vapour) from the soil and condense (turn back into liquid from vapour) on the lid and sides of the container. On warm days, the inside of the containers will appear misty because of the water vapour in the air. This is a simulation of the same water cycle that goes on continuously in the Earth's atmosphere.

In the terrarium, once the seeds germinate and produce a vegetative cover over the soil less water should be able to evaporate. Having the two mini-systems lets you see quite how much of an effect the vegetation has. The system without the plants demonstrates what would happen to ecosystems if vegetation were removed (as in deforestation), and how the climate may be more extreme in their absence.

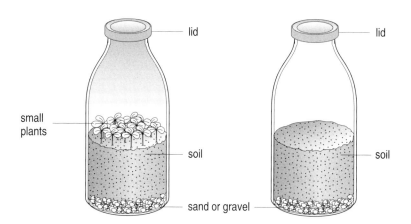

Extension ideas

Add a small dish of salty water into the terrarium. On warm days the water will evaporate leaving the salt visible in the dish. This shows that salt remains in the sea and pure water will evaporate to form clouds and eventually rain.

Place a stick of chalk or an iron nail upright in the terrarium and watch the effect of weathering on these items. Water will erode these structures. Graveyards are great places for observing this since there should be some very old structures here, and the headstones are dated making it easy to see erosion over time.

This experiment was recommended to us by...

The team at Science Line – ring them free on 0808 800 4000 or access the website at *www.sciencenet.org.uk*

National Curriculum links in KS2

Sc3 2e, Sc2 3a-d (Green plants), Sc2 5a, Sc3 1e, Sc3 2d. The experiment can cover much of Sc1, especially obtaining and presenting evidence (Sc1 2d and Sc1 2e–h).

Looking forward – National Curriculum links in KS3

Again, there are links to the Sc2 curriculum on green plants including the KS3 topic of photosynthesis. Also in terms of Sc2, environmental protection issues can be discussed, which for KS3 include the importance of sustainable development. In terms of Sc3, changes of state (evaporation, condensation etc.) are developed into thinking in terms of particles getting further or closer together. As above, the experiment provides many opportunities to cover Sc1.

Give it a pasting

An investigation to get your teeth into, with D&T links as well as science

Setting the scene

In advance, ask the pupils to bring in toothpaste, toothpaste boxes and adverts. Ask the pupils what sort of things toothpaste needs to do (e.g. neutralize acids, make a lather to help with cleaning). Once the pupils have worked out a criteria for good toothpaste, they can get into pairs and design an investigation to compare one brand against the other.

You will need

- Toothpaste. The pupils plan the investigation themselves, so they will determine the equipment.

Instructions

None! But a few ideas you could suggest and prepare for:

- Check the ingredients on the packet. Test how much they lather – mix water and toothpaste in a test-tube then shake up and down and finally measure the height of the foam.

- Test the acidity of the toothpaste. Toothpaste helps to get rid of acids (in fruit juice, etc.) so it needs to be alkaline. To test this the pupils will need indicator paper and a key.

- Each test should be done at least twice – once for each kind of toothpaste. To ensure the test is 'fair', the conditions for the first toothpaste test must be the same for the second.

Extension ideas

Try comparing 'normal' to speciality toothpastes like sensitive or baby's. For D&T, ask the pupils to design their own toothpaste boxes and adverts, with science/dentistry as a selling point.

This experiment was recommended to us by...

Sue Worley, ex-science teacher. Thanks to the Institute of Biology for putting us in contact with her.

National Curriculum links in KS2

Sc1 2d (much else in Sc1 can be covered too), Sc2 2a.

Looking forward – National Curriculum links in KS3

Again, it's main curriculum relevance lies in Sc1, especially 'planning' (Sc1 2a–e) which is developed in KS3 to include thinking about variables (Sc1 2d).

Remember BE SAFE: If pupils use disclosing tablets make sure they bring and use his/her own toothbrush. Soak toothbrushes in a sterilising solution such as 'Milton' for 30 minutes before use. (*Be Safe!*, 3rd edition, section 12)

The Little Book of Experiments

Bad-breath!
Fire-fighting and dangerous gases – all from the kitchen

Setting the scene

Ask the class to breathe deeply in and then out. Explain that air is a mix of different gases and that we breathe in oxygen and then breathe out carbon dioxide (CO_2). Fire – like animals – needs oxygen to stay alive or burn.

- Pint jug (anything with a lip you can pour from),
- Small candle (e.g. night-light) and matches,
- Vinegar, hot water and baking soda.

- Prepare a hot water – from a tap is fine – and vinegar mix, (fifty-fifty of each).
- Light the candle.
- Put about a dessertspoon of baking powder in your jug, then pour on the water-vinegar mix.
- Let the fizz subside for a second or so, then take the jug and 'pour' the CO_2 over the candle. It will go out, 'suffocated' by the lack of oxygen.

CO_2 is heavier than air, so when you lean the jug over the candle CO_2 falls out and sinks onto the flame extinguishing it.

Where CO_2 issues from the ground in high concentrations it stays low and in sheltered areas it has killed birds, mice and cats. In Cameroon, a sudden efflux of CO_2 from under a lake flooded a village and all the people died.

Professor Paul Jarvis (FRS), the University of Edinburgh.

Sc2 5a, Sc3 2a, Sc3 2f, Sc4 2b.

This experiment links to the concept of chemical reactions, especially 'elements, compounds and mixtures' (Sc3 1c–h) and 'physical changes' (Sc3 2a–c). You can also discuss protecting the environment (Sc2 5a and Sc3 2i).

Remember BE SAFE: About heating and burning anything! (*Be Safe!*, 3rd edition, section 8 & 9)

Cereal Chemist

How exactly do they 'fortify' breakfast cereals with all that iron?

You will need

- Branflakes,
- A high-sided plastic container (e.g. a large yoghurt pot),
- Magnet,
- Clingfilm,
- Wooden spoon.

Instructions

Crush the branflakes. Now turn your wooden spoon into a magnet-spoon – stick a magnet on the bottom of the spoon and cover it over by wrapping clingfilm around the spoon and magnet.

Stir the bran flakes with the magnet spoon for 10 minutes (you may want to pass this round a group of pupils). Wash off any excess branflakes on the spoon and look to see what is left on the cling film. You should see little bits of metal by the magnet. These are the added iron in the bran flakes – yes honest, they really use iron filings!

Further information

Different brands have different amounts of iron. If at first you don't succeed, you might find this useful. Stretch the clingfilm out (you will need two people, one holding either side). Shake the crushed branflakes on top of the clingfilm and hold the magnet underneath it. Blow away the bran flakes and the iron filings will be left on the bit of clingfilm that's next to the magnet.

This experiment was recommended to us by...

From Dr Graeme Jones, Chemistry Department of Keele University. The alternative version is from the Year 5 & 6 students at The Edward Richardson Primary School, Tetford.

National Curriculum links in KS2

Sc4 2a. It also relates to separating mixtures of materials (Sc3 3a–e) and touches on ideas and evidence in science (Sc1 1a–b).

Looking forward – National Curriculum links in KS3

Links to much of the KS3 curriculum on nutrition (Sc2 2a–d), as well as work on classifying materials (Sc3 1g) – although much of this in KS3 goes more towards particulate theory.

Remember BE SAFE: Don't let the pupils eat the branflakes! (*Be Safe!*, 3rd edition, section 6)

Make a Fossil

It takes thousands of years to create a fossil but you can do it in a week!

You will need

- A light plastic container to make the fossil in (e.g. a yoghurt pot or a fruit punnet),
- A sponge (any kind but the more holes the better),
- Some fine sand (enough to half fill your container),
- Bath salts,
- A saucer or small tray.

Instructions

- Create a shape from your fossil by cutting it out from the sponge – it could be a shell, a bone or a whole dinosaur.
- Make a couple of small holes in the bottom of your container. Place it on a saucer or tray as you're going to pour water over it and you don't want it to spill!
- Put some sand in the container about a 1 cm of the way up and then place your sponge body on top and cover with another 2 cm of sand.
- Mix 4 tablespoons of bath salts in 4 tablespoons of warm water and pour over the cup, letting the mix sink through the sand. Leave it somewhere safe and warm (e.g. a window ledge).
- Replenish the water and salt mix at least once a day for at least five days. The longer you leave it the more fossilised it becomes.
- Leave the sand to dry out for two days before removing the 'fossil' sponge. If it's still a little wet, leave the fossil for a few days before handling it.
- The holes in the sponge trap the salts, mineralising the sponge, as they dry out it solidifies to create a fossil.

This experiment was recommended to us by...

Clare Eastup, an ex-geologist who now works in the very geology-free (but still great!) Museum of Science and Industry, Manchester.

National Curriculum links in KS2

Sc3 1d, and also to Geography 4b (recognising some physical and human processes).

Looking forward – National Curriculum links in KS3

Geology is greatly developed in the KS3 Sc3 curriculum. This experiment links to the section on 'geological changes' (Sc3 2d–f). The experiment also relates to 'knowledge and understanding of environmental change and sustainable development' (5a in the Geography curriculum).

Planet Science

Custard gone Crazy

Is it a solid? Is a liquid? No, it's Planet Science's favourite trick!

You will need:

- Custard powder (or cornflour – but not instant custard powder),
- Water,
- Eggcup,
- Bowl,
- Spoon.

Instructions

Mix 8 eggcups of custard powder with 4 eggcups of water, making sure to stir in the water a little at a time so you don't get any lumps. The result is a strange yellow substance that can act either like a solid (if you punch it quickly or roll it into a ball) or like a liquid (if you touch it gently). Weird.

If you increase the amounts of custard and water, you could in theory fill a paddling pool with the mixture, and run across the top without falling in. (If you do this you can jump up and down, but when you stop jumping you sink into the mixture. To remove your feet pull gently or you may be stuck there for good!)

Further information

When you move the custard mix around slowly the custard powder particles can move around in the water quite freely, and so it acts as a liquid. When you move the mix faster or hold it in your hand tightly, the solid particles rub against each other causing friction. This makes them stick together and act like a solid.

This experiment was recommended to us by…

Us! It was part of the Science Year 'Put Your Teacher On The Spot' campaign, as featured on TV and in cinemas.

National Curriculum Links in KS2

Sc3 3b, Sc3 3e.

Looking forward – National Curriculum links in KS3

Underpins aspects of 'solids, liquids and gases' (Sc3 1a–b) and 'elements, compounds and mixtures'(Sc3 1c–h). Also 'how friction effects motion' (Sc4 2d).

Remember BE SAFE: Don't let the pupils eat the custard! (*Be Safe!*, 3rd edition, section 6)

The Little Book of Experiments

Dancing Paper
A great trick to encourage pupils to think about attraction and repulsion

You will need

★ Paper 'confetti' (the stuff that comes out the bottom of a hole-punch is ideal),

★ Some sort of plastic box. It's important that it's not too deep and has a clear plastic lid (e.g. an empty audio-tape cassette box or some types of chocolate boxes),

★ A piece of cloth (board rubbers work well).

Instructions

★ Put your 'confetti' into the plastic box.

★ Rub the top quickly with a **dry** hand or a piece of cloth.

★ Watch the confetti dance up and down.

Further information

Rubbing the top of the clear plastic box 'charges' it electrically and it attracts the small pieces of paper. When these touch the top of the box they pick up the same charge and are pushed away again. Losing their charge when they touch the bottom of the box, they are attracted once again...

This experiment was recommended to us by...

Ian Russell

National Curriculum links in KS2

Sc4 2a (if you link electricity to magnetism).

Looking forward – National Curriculum links in KS3

Relates to aspects of particulate theory (Sc3 1a), and 'magnetic fields' (Sc4 1d).

Goose-pimples
The difference between things happening all over your body or just in one place

You will need

- A cold day (teeth-chatteringly so),
- Large bowl of warm water (as warm as a bath),
- Bunch of victims in shirtsleeves.

Instructions

- First you need to introduce the experiment to the class by posing the following question. Goose-pimples are a response to cold – but are they **systemic** or **local**? That is, do they affect your whole body or just the bits that are cold?
- Get a child covered in goose-pimples to put their arm under the surface of the warm water – do the goose-pimples disappear in this area?

Further information

The answer is that at first you still have goose-pimples under the surface of warm water, so they must be a whole body reaction. Obviously as the warm water warms all your blood, they'll disappear, but they'll disappear everywhere.

This experiment was recommended to us by...

Dr John McLachlan, Peninsula Medical School, Plymouth.

National Curriculum links in KS2

'Ideas and evidence in science' (Sc2 2c, Sc1 a–b) and other aspects of Sc1 (especially 2a, 2b, 2g, 3k, 3l).

Looking forward – National Curriculum links in KS3

Because the experiment gets the pupils to think about circulation within their own bodies, it underpins much of 'humans as organisms' (Sc2 2a–n). It also relates to aspects of the curriculum concerning 'adaptation and inheritance' (Sc2 4 and 5).

Ketchup Sachet
A simple science toy that's been around for centuries

You will need

- 2 litre plastic bottle,
- A sachet of ketchup,
- Sachets of other sauces to experiment with (optional).

Instructions

- Fill the bottle full of water. Put the sachet in the top and secure the lid on. When you squeeze the bottle the sachet dives down into the bottle – let go and it'll float back up.

Further information

An object will only sink if it is denser that the fluid around it, otherwise it floats. The ketchup is denser than water, so should sink. But your sachet of ketchup is actually ketchup plus packaging plus an air bubble, so overall it is less dense than ketchup on its own, and floats somewhere around the middle of your bottle.

Press the sides of the bottle and you'll make the volume of the bottle smaller. Everything inside the bottle is compressed (squashed). Gases compress easily compared to liquids, so it is the air bubble inside your sachet that gets squashed the most. Now the air bubble is denser, so your ketchup plus packaging plus an air bubble is also denser than before therefore isn't as buoyant (floatable) and so sinks.

This experiment was recommended to us by...

Graham Dolan of the Royal Observatory, Greenwich and his colleagues at the National Maritime Museum. It also featured in the Science Year 'Put Your Teacher On The Spot' campaign.

National Curriculum links in KS2

Links to aspects of Sc1, but the scientific principles covered here do not really enter into the curriculum at KS2.

Looking forward – National Curriculum links in KS3

This links to 'the relationship between force area and pressure' (Sc4 2g) and underpins aspects of the Sc3 curriculum relating to 'densities' (Sc3 1a–b).

Magic Milk-bottles

How can an egg be made to go through the neck of a bottle?

You will need

- A milk bottle,
- Matches,
- Scrap paper for burning,
- Water-bomb (filled).

Instructions

- Set fire to a small piece of newspaper, drop the lighted paper into the bottle and immediately put the water bomb on the mouth of the bottle. It will then get pulled in (emitting a divine and slightly rude noise) to general gasps of amazement all round.

- It also works with a hardboiled (shelled!) egg. But it's easier to get the water-bomb out of the bottle when your finished, and the water-bomb is supposed to make a ruder noise (not that we'd care about that).

Further information

The burning paper burns away some of the oxygen thus creating a partial vacuum in the bottle (that is, the air inside the bottle shrinks). As the air pressure outside the bottle is now greater, the balloon gets forced into the bottle.

This experiment was recommended to us by...

Judy Vincent, science teacher, who was shown the experiment at an ASE conference and never forgot it and by a student, Roy Garner, the winner of our 'Science Year Shorts' short film competition. You can see this experiment on-line as part of our 'Put Your Teacher on the Spot' experiment series.

National Curriculum links in KS2

Sc1 1a, Sc1 2b, Sc1 2l, Sc4 2e.

Looking forward – National Curriculum links in KS3

'The relationship between force area and pressure' (Sc4 2g), also aspects of Sc3 in relation to 'changes of state' (Sc3 1b).

Remember BE SAFE: With any flames, ensure there is water, sand or a fire blanket available in case anything goes wrong! (*Be Safe!*, 3rd edition, section 8)

The Little Book of Experiments

Make a Menagerie

Use your imaginations to come up with a load of unreal but possible animals

Setting the Scene

Using nature documentaries, books and/or the web, show the class contrasting habitats and the sort of animals that live in them. Get the class to discuss the ways the animals fit their habitats, and emphasis the impact of environment on the evolution of the animal.

What you need

Because it's about what 'could be' not 'what is', you won't need any fancy equipment – just paper, crayons and access to a library.

Instructions

- Make up a type of habitat and write a short description on the board telling the class the sort of conditions an animal of this habitat would live in. This could be real, or on a made-up planet, or imagine drastic climate change creating a rainforest in Yorkshire.

- The pupils need to design a new animal that has adapted to live in your habitat. You can also get the pupils to make a fact sheet about their new creature, and a bestiary of the whole class's incredible beasts makes for a great display.

This experiment was recommended to us by…

Janine Phillips and the rest of the education team at London Zoo.

National Curriculum links in KS2

Sc2 1a, Sc2 1c, Sc1 2h, Sc2 5b, Sc2 5c.

Looking forward – National Curriculum links in KS3

As above, this experiment relates to much of the curriculum concerning 'variation, classification and inheritance' (Sc2 4a–c) and 'living things and their environment' (Sc2 5a–f).

Planet Science

Rotting eggs and rotten teeth

How can we test the effects of cola on teeth without actually damaging some in the process – cheat!

You will need

★ Some eggshell,
★ A glass,
★ A selection of soft-drinks (e.g. cola, squash, a juice-drink, fresh fruit juice and water).

Instructions

★ Hang a bit of eggshell from a thread, and suspend it in a glass. Fill the glass with cola. Do the same in other glasses but with squash, juice-drink, fresh fruit juice and water. Leave them for a week, then remove the eggshell fragments for comparison.

squash   juice drink   fresh fruit juice   water   eggshell

★ The cola shell will be soft to the touch, the squash and juice-drink shells will also be soft (although not necessarily as much) and the juice and water ones should be undamaged.

★ Now for the 'yuk' bit – the experiment would have had the same effect if you'd used human teeth instead of eggshells! Try it, if your pupils are at the milk-teeth falling out stage (and willing to forgo a tooth-fairy visit for the sake of science), but eggshells are made of a similar material to teeth so make a great alternative.

This experiment was recommended to us by…

Sue Brumpton of The Making Place, a hands-on science and technology centre in West London.

National Curriculum links in KS2

Sc2 2a, Sc2 2b.

Looking forward – National Curriculum links in KS3

As above, this links to the aspects of the Sc2 curriculum concerning 'human health', although at KS3 the functions and care of teeth are not specifically covered.

Remember BE SAFE: Any teeth will have to be sterilised before handling and make sure the eggshells are clean! (*Be Safe!*, 3rd edition, section 11)

The Little Book of Experiments   55

It's a Gas!
Use drama to explain changes of state – your pupils are the particles

You will need

- A large clear space,
- Children!

Instructions

Clear the classroom or go into the playground. This space is your mug, half full of water (you might want to chalk up a half-mark). The class is the water – each pupil is an H_2O molecule. A nice idea is to have a 'magic ray gun', to zap energy into the class (and freeze it out).

As a solid, all pupils stand in rows, shoulder to shoulder. They must vibrate (jig on the spot, do the twist, hop up and down) but not stand still – this would be 'absolute zero'. As the temperature increases, the vibrations become bigger until pupils can break from the more ordered solid structure (melt) and go wherever they want around the bottom half of the 'mug', but they must have at least one arm linked to another pupil.

As they turn into a gas, the kinetic energy (movement) of the molecules increases until the molecules have enough energy to fill the entire mug. The pupils walk in straight lines until they hit either another pupil or the edge of the mug – then rebound off like pool-balls off a side cushion.

You can also label-up some of the class as tea, milk and sugar molecules and work through dissolving by turning them into a cup of tea.

This experiment was recommended to us by...

Ped Saunders, teacher at Bradwell Village Middle School, Milton Keynes.

National Curriculum links in KS2

Sc3 1e, Sc3 2a, Sc3 2b, Sc3 2d, Sc3 2f, Sc3 3b.

Looking forward – National Curriculum links in KS3

This experiment lays the ground well for thinking in terms of particles, an idea which underpins much of KS3 Sc3 (especially Sc3 1a–b).

Blowing in the Wind

Build a forest strong enough to withstand a strong wind

You will need (enough for each group)

- Paper,
- Glue,
- Tape,
- Scissors,
- Something to imitate wind (e.g. hair dryer).

Instructions

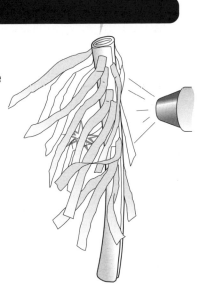

- Divide the class into small groups. Give each group five sheets of paper, glue, tape and scissors. Each group must make a sturdy tree. However (just to be tricky) they also have to make the trees as tall as possible to compete for sunlight, and with good leaf cover to maximise photosynthesis.

- Put all the trees together to make a forest. The pupils can compare their trees with the others, and look at the differences. There are three criteria for judgement – staying power against the wind, height and leaf coverage. The children will have had to make decisions and compromises.

- Now test the trees against the 'wind'. You can build this up and vary it with different sources – hair dryers, electric fans, a board flapped to make a slight breeze, or all of them together to create a gale!

This experiment was recommended to us by…

Lesley Wood, teacher at Portway Junior School, Andover.

National Curriculum links in KS2

Sc2 3a–c, Sc2 5b–c, and Sc1 (especially 2c, 2d, 2i, 2k, 2m).

Looking forward – National Curriculum links in KS3

As above, this experiment relates to much of the curriculum concerning 'variation, classification and inheritance' (Sc2 4a–c) and 'living things and their environment' (Sc2 5a–f), as well as the section on 'green plants as organisms' (Sc2 3a–e). Again, this investigation can be used to cover much of Sc1, especially the planning (Sc1 2a–e) and evaluating (Sc1 2n–p) sections.

Remember BE SAFE: Any electrical equipment must have passed the portable electrical appliance test, even if it's been brought in from home! Make sure any moving fan blades are adequately guarded. (*Be Safe!*, 3rd edition, section 10)

Planetary Plates

Explore the planets (with a bit of help from the crockery cupboard)

You will need

- ★ Different sized plates, ask each child to bring one from home (with their parents permission, of course),
- ★ Ruler,
- ★ Tape measure.

Instructions

- ★ Get the pupils to measure the diameter of their plate, and write the measurement onto a wall chart.
- ★ Take the largest plate and mount it on the wall. (If it is really heavy you might need to make a card replica that you can stick on the wall instead.) Draw a straight line on the floor in front of the plate, and ask each pupil to stand on the line holding their plate.
- ★ How far from the mounted plate do they need to stand in order to completely obscure it with their plate. Measure the distance between the two plates and write this measurement on a new column on the wall chart.
- ★ Can you see a relationship between the columns of numbers? How can this help us to understand eclipses? It's also worth using cotton to measure the circumference of the plate. Write this on your chart, and divide the circumference by the diameter. What do you notice?

National Curriculum links in KS2

'The Earth and beyond' (Sc4 4a–d) and much of Sc1 can be covered (depending on how you treat it). Links to Mathematics include most of Ma3 (space and measurement) and Ma4 (handling data).

Looking forward – National Curriculum links in KS3

'The Solar system' (Sc4 4a–c) and most of Sc1 is relevant for investigative skills. The links to Mathematics are 'using and applying shape, space and measures' (Ma3). The experiment can also be developed to include use of 'coordinates' (Ma3 3e).

Pinhole Camera

Make a camera obscura, and help find out how the eye works

You will need

- A small cardboard box, with thin sides (like a box for tea),
- A sharp pencil,
- Tracing paper,
- Sticky tape,
- Scissors,
- Black paint, magnifying glass (both optional).

Instructions

- Assuming your box is not square, select one of the larger sides and draw a frame 2 cm in from each side. Cut out the inner rectangle and remove.

- Paint the inside of the box black and allow to dry. Cut out a piece of tracing paper and stick it across the missing side to form a window. Make a small hole in the side opposite the tracing paper window.

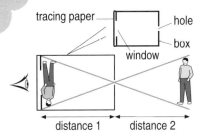

- Direct the hole towards a brightly lit object and look at the window. You should see an upside-down image in the window. If the image is too dark make the hole larger (1 cm across is ideal), however the image will be more blurred. Use the magnifying glass to focus the image.

The pinhole camera works like the eye. The hole is the pupil, the tracing paper is the retina, and the magnifying glass is the lens.

Extension ideas

On a sunny day, darken your classroom, make a small hole in the blind and look at the opposite wall. If there is a view outside you should see an upside down version of it.

This experiment was recommended to us by...

Sophie Duncan, ex-Planet Science staff and a great maker of pinhole cameras.

National Curriculum links in KS2

Sc4 3a–b, Sc4 3d.

Looking forward – National Curriculum links in KS3

In the KS3 curriculum for light, it is very important to emphasise that light travels in straight lines. You can help pupils see this as part of the experiment by getting them to draw diagrams of the camera and draw on how the light travels around it.

The Little Book of Experiments

Pressurised Plastic
'Feel the force' and demonstrate air pressure

You will need

- Metal bowl (thick ceramic works too – the idea is to have something strong),
- Plastic bag that is slightly bigger than the bowl,
- Thick elastic band.

Instructions

- Open the bag up and use it to line the inside of the bowl (you want the opening of the bag to go round the bowl's rim). Then pull the elastic band securely around the edge of the bowl to seal the plastic bag to the bowl's rim.

- Now offer the bag and bowl to a willing volunteer and ask them to pull the bag out of the bottom of the bowl. Any attempt to do so produces very low air pressure between the bag and the bowl. This is opposed by the pressure outside the bowl, so it is very hard to pull the bag out.

- This helps the audience to understand atmospheric pressure, which they do not usually feel as it is always present, and also the strength that air pressure can have. It's these sorts of air pressures that are behind aeroplanes flying.

This experiment was recommended to us by...

Adam Love-Rogers at the Royal Air Force Museum, Hendon.

National Curriculum links in KS2

Links to 'forces and motion' (Sc4 2), 'ideas and evidence in science' (Sc1 1a–b), and Sc1 2l.

Looking forward – National Curriculum links in KS3

This links to 'ways in which frictional forces affect motion' (Sc4 2d), it also relates to 'the relationship between force, area and pressure' (Sc4 2g).

Light Fantastic
Impact on pupils' understanding of a green plant's need for light

You will need

- 3 identical small plants in pots,
- 3 large plastic drinks bottles (1 black, 1 brown and 1 clear),
- 3 saucers.

Instructions

- Cut the drinks bottles in half so that the bottoms of them fit comfortably over the plant. Put the plants on the saucers and the bottles over the plants. Keep them a week, watering them regularly, but remember to give each plant exactly the same amount of water as the others.

- After a week remove the covers and note the differences. Depending of the age of the plants at the start of the experiment, the one without any light is frequently in a state of complete collapse. The effects on the plants of different levels of light are quite dramatic and cause thought-provoking reactions which are never forgotten.

clear   black   brown

Extension ideas

Cut shapes of stars, moons and suns out of cardboard and weigh them down (gently enough not to damage the grass but heavy enough for the shapes not to blow off). Leave in the sun for a few days and then lift. There'll be patches of pale grass where your shapes blocked the sun. Without the sunlight the plants cannot make the chemical they need to look green.

This experiment was recommended to us by...

Gwyneth Irvine, Year 6 teacher at Stickland's School, Evershot. The extension idea came from Helen Story – a fashion designer who's looked extensively at scientific themes in her work.

National Curriculum links in KS2

Sc2 3a, Sc 1b. Aspects of Sc1 can be covered.

Looking forward – National Curriculum links in KS3

This is a good experiment to introduce pupils to photosynthesis. It also links to 'green plants as organisms' (Sc2 3e) and 'living things and their environment' (Sc2 5a–f).

The Little Book of Experiments

Whether the weather will...
Is melting ice making the sea 'overflow'?

You will need

- A glass,
- Ice,
- Marker pen,
- Ruler.

Instructions

- Fill a glass three-quarters full with water and add ice. Mark with your marker pen a line along the water level and measure the height from the bottom of the glass to the line, then wait for the ice to melt...

- Once the ice melts, mark the new water level line and measure the new height from the bottom of the glass to the line. There should be a small drop in water level, as ice (unlike most other things) is actually **bigger** in its solid form that in its liquid form, and so shrinks as it melts!

- To test this, put some water into a plastic beaker so that it is one third full. Mark the water level and put it into a freezer. When you remove the beaker the level of ice will be higher than your line.

Further information

So, the result of this experiment means the polar ice-caps have nothing to do with rising sea-levels – but global warming **does** lead to a rise in sea-level. This is because even though H_2O is unusual and expands when it freezes, it still expands as it warms. The global rise in temperature has meant the water in our seas has got bigger, and so the overall global sea level has risen because of it.

This experiment was recommended to us by...

Dr Simon Torok, the Tyndall Centre for Climate Change Research.

National Curriculum links in KS2

Sc3 2b, can also be extended into Sc2 5a.

Looking forward – National Curriculum links in KS3

Sc3, especially 'solid, liquids and gases' (Sc3 1a–b) and 'physical changes' (2a–c). Also links to protecting the environment (which in KS3 is developed into the idea of sustainable development, Sc2 5a and Sc3 2i).

The Great Boat Race

Run your own boat race and discover the best shape for a boat

You will need:

- Thin timber,
- Piece of plastic guttering 2 m long,
- Piece of cotton 2 m long,
- Small weight,
- Glue.

Instructions

- Using the timber make a number of different boats, all with different shaped fronts. Ask the children which boat they think would move quickest through the water, making sure you emphasise that they are making a prediction you're going to test out.
- Take the guttering and raise it onto a high flat surface (e.g. use some clamps on a table). Attach one end of the cotton to the boat and the other end to the weight. Place the boat in the water near to one end of the guttering, and allow the weight to hang over the opposite end of the guttering. Let go of the weight. As it falls the boat is pulled through the water. Time how long it takes for each boat to move through the water.
- Work out why some boats are faster than others. This can lead to interesting discussions about forces and water resistance.

This experiment was recommended to us by…

Keith Weston, Ditchingham Primary School, Norfolk.

National Curriculum links in KS2

Sc4 2c, also Sc1 investigative skills.

Looking forward – National Curriculum links in KS3

As above, this is an investigation so can be used to cover much of Sc1. It also relates to Sc4, especially aspects of 'force and linear motion' (Sc4 2a–d).

Seed-tastic!
Learn about seed dispersal, with a bit of physics thrown in too

You will need (per group)

- Paper,
- Sticky tape,
- 10 g masses (or pennies or marbles should do, as long as everyone in the class has the same mass).

Instructions

- Split the class into small groups. Each group has to design 'seeds' using the paper and sticky tape. The 10 g mass is the seed-pod.

- Once designed, drop the seeds (preferably from a height). The challenge is to get the seed to stay in the air as long as possible and travel as far as possible.

- The pupils can make star shapes, cross shapes, cones and 'parachutes'. This is a great experiment for being creative. You can do it as a competitive challenge, or as a more structured investigation if you decide the shapes in advance.

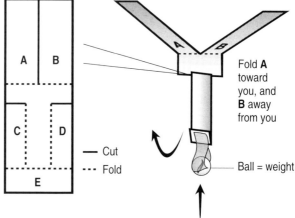

This experiment was recommended to us by...

Jeremy Thomas, teacher at Launceston College in Cornwall.

National Curriculum links in KS2

Sc4 2b, Sc4 2c, most of Sc1 can be covered depending on how the investigative aspect of the activity is treated by the teacher.

Looking forward – National Curriculum links in KS3

As above, this investigation can be used to cover much of Sc1. It also relates to much of 'force and linear motion' in the KS3 curriculum on 'forces and motion' (Sc4 2a–d) It can also be linked to aspects of Sc2 concerning the reproduction of plants and their relationship to the environment.

Remember BE SAFE: Avoid children standing on tables to drop their seeds. If you want them to gain height, for example by using a climbing frame, make sure they are appropriately supervised. (*Be Safe!*, 3rd edition, section 5)